God had special plans for Joseph.

When Joseph was a boy, his father taught him how to pray and how to work.

Joseph learned to choose sturdy wood. He learned to measure it, cut it with saws and nail it together. He practised again and again, until he could use his tools without cutting his fingers and make the wood so smooth he did not get splinters.

Joseph also learned to pray the Psalms. He learned to follow God's laws, the Ten Commandments that God had given to Moses. He practised again and again, and learned to love God with all his mind and all his heart and all his strength.

'Help me to do the things that are good and kind,' Joseph asked God. And he did. He grew up into a good, kind man with a carpenter's hands.

When Joseph was grown up, he met a young woman named Mary. He offered her his hands, rough and calloused from good, honest work. They were also strong, gentle hands. He wanted to use them to care for Mary. Her family was pleased, and Joseph and Mary planned the day when they would be married.

9

A little while before their wedding, Mary came to Joseph.

'Joseph,' she said, 'I'm going to have a baby.'

Joseph was confused and troubled. He had always wanted to please God and do what was right. He loved Mary and wanted her to be his wife. He would do nothing to hurt her or harm her. But how could there be a baby?

11

When Joseph was alone, he did what he always did when he was confused and troubled. He put his hands together and he prayed.

'Father God,' he said, 'what should I do? How can I do what is right and good?'

Joseph felt very tired. He was still thinking about Mary and her baby when he fell asleep.

13

God answered Joseph's prayers. Joseph dreamed. And in his dream, he saw an angel who gave him a message from God himself.

'Don't be afraid, Joseph. Mary is good and kind.
She has done nothing wrong. God wants you to marry her and look after her. Her baby is God's own Son, conceived by the Holy Spirit. You will call him Jesus.'

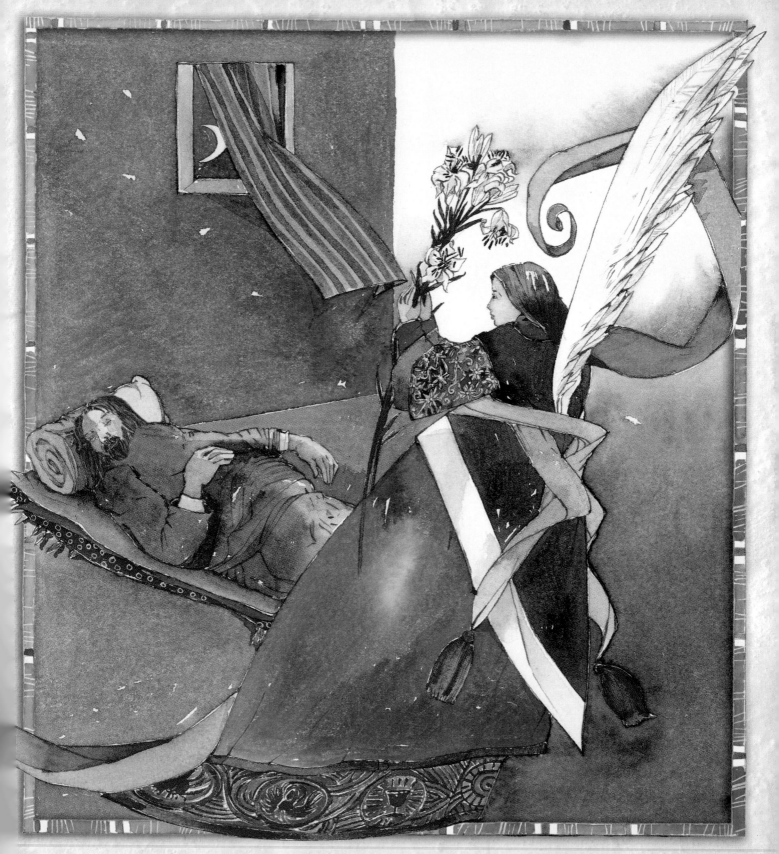

When Joseph woke up, he knew that God had spoken to him. He understood that Mary's baby was very special and that he, Joseph, had been given a special job to do.

Joseph took Mary home as his wife. Together they prepared for the birth of her baby, the baby they would call Jesus.

17

Some months later, the Roman emperor decided that there would be a census of all his people. Everyone had to return to the home of their ancestors to be counted.

Joseph was a descendant of King David, so he prepared with Mary to go to Bethlehem, a journey of several days. Joseph helped Mary on to the donkey for their journey to Bethlehem. Together they travelled with many others along dusty roads.

19

When they arrived in Bethlehem, Joseph knocked on doors.

He hoped to find a room, a place where they could stay after their journey.

Joseph knew that God had given him this job, to protect and care for Mary, as the pains came that told her that soon she would give birth to her baby son.

It was a starry night when Joseph placed clean hay in a manger and made ready a place for Mary's baby.

Joseph stayed with Mary until finally he held God's Son, Jesus, the promised Saviour, with hands as strong and gentle and tender as any father's hands.

Joseph prayed again:

'Father God, now more than ever, help me to do what is right and good for this holy, precious child.'

23

Mary and Joseph did not get much sleep that night. Joseph listened with Mary as shepherds, excited and full of the news of the baby's birth, came to visit them.

Joseph heard about the angels, who had appeared to the shepherds on the hillside and told them that Jesus had been born and where to go to find him. The echoes of the angels' song seemed to come with the shepherds to Bethlehem:

'Praise God in heaven! Peace on earth to everyone…'

On another starry night, Joseph watched in wonder as camels stopped outside the door of a little house in Bethlehem. Wise men entered, bringing gifts for Jesus, whom they called a baby king.

Joseph saw the men worship the child he helped to care for. When they left, he held in his hands the gifts they had left-—gold, frankincense and myrrh—and put them safely away.

That night God sent his angel to Joseph in another dream.

'Take the child and his mother to Egypt, for Herod means to kill him! Stay there until I tell you it is safe to return.'

J Joseph protected Mary and Jesus as they left
Bethlehem by night and travelled to Egypt. Joseph
provided them with food, shelter and safety while they
made their home in a foreign land until God sent his
angel in a third dream.

'Return to Israel, Joseph. The people who were
seeking the child's life are dead.'

Joseph took Mary and Jesus to Israel and to a
home in Nazareth where, just like his own father,
Joseph taught Jesus how to pray and how to
work.

Joseph, Mary and Jesus were all safely in
God's hands, part of a greater plan.

Published by
The Bible Reading Fellowship
15 The Chambers, Vineyard
Abingdon, OX14 3FE
United Kingdom
Tel: +44 (0)1865 319700
Email: enquiries@brf.org.uk
Website: www.brf.org.uk
BRF is a Registered Charity

ISBN 978 1 84101 822 5

First edition 2010

Publishing Director: Annette Reynolds
Art Director: Gerald Rogers
Pre-production Manager: Krystyna Kowalska Hewitt
Production Manager: John Laister

Printed and bound in Singapore